thanks

These quotations were gathered lovingly but unscientifically over several years and/or contributed by many friends or acquaintances. Some arrived, and survived in our files, on scraps of paper and may therefore be imperfectly worded or attributed. To the authors, contributors and original sources, our thanks, and where appropriate, our apologies.—The editors

C R E D I T S

Compiled by Kobi Yamada
Designed by Steve Potter

ISBN: 1-888387-70-X

Printed in China

Thank you for being.

NATIVE AMERICAN GREETING

Some people
make the world
more special
just by
being in it.

KELLY ANN ROTHAUS

PEOPLE WHO
DEAL WITH LIFE GENEROUSLY
AND LARGE-HEARTEDLY
GO ON MULTIPLYING
RELATIONSHIPS
TO THE END.

ARTHUR CHRISTOPHER BENSON

You never know

when a moment

and a few sincere

words can have an

impact on a life.

ZIG ZIGLAR

IT'S THE LITTLE THINGS IN LIFE
THAT LEAD TO THE BIG.

ROSE ZADRA

The thoughtful
little things
you do each day
have an
accumulated effect
on all our tomorrows.

ALEXANDRA STODDARD

WE MUST FIND TIME
TO STOP
AND THANK THE PEOPLE
WHO MAKE
A DIFFERENCE IN
OUR LIVES.

ROBERT KENNEDY

Just as there are

no little people

or unimportant

lives, there is no

insignificant work.

ELENA BONNER

If someone
listens,
or stretches
out a hand,
or whispers
a kind word of
encouragement,
or attempts to
understand,
extraordinary
things
begin to happen.

LORETTA GIRZARTIS

I am beginning

to learn that

it is the sweet,

simple things of life

which are the

real ones after all.

LAURA INGALLS WILDER

It's a great satisfaction knowing that for a brief point in time you made a difference.

IRENE NATIVIDAD

UNSELFISH ACTS

ARE THE

REAL MIRACLES

OUT OF WHICH ALL

THE REPORTED

MIRACLES GROW.

RALPH WALDO EMERSON

There is in each
of us so much
goodness that
if we could see
its glow, it would
light the world.

SAM FRIEND

THE EFFECT OF ONE GOOD-HEARTED PERSON
IS INCALCULABLE.

OSCAR ARIAS

Sometimes
our light goes out
but is blown
into flame
by another
human being.
Each of us
owes deepest thanks
to those who have
rekindled
this light.

ALBERT SCHWEITZER

I GET BY WITH A LITTLE HELP
FROM MY FRIENDS.

JOHN LENNON

It is one of the most beautiful compensations of this life that you cannot sincerely try to help another without helping yourself.

RALPH WALDO EMERSON

It is in the shelter

of each other

that the people live.

IRISH PROVERB

WHERE WOULD
ANY OF US
BE WITHOUT OUR
FAMILY
AND FRIENDS?

KOBI YAMADA

Strange, isn't it

George, how each

man's life touches

so many others,

and when he isn't

around it leaves

an awful hole.

CLARENCE THE ANGEL
"IT'S A WONDERFUL LIFE"

The people you meet become a part of you. They leave their imprints not just on you, but inside you.

JOYCE MACINTOSH

Life is not a path
of coincidence,
happenstance,
and luck, but rather
an unexplainable,
meticulously charted
course for one to touch
the lives of
others and make a
difference in the world.

BARBARA DILLINHAM

Let your friends,

colleagues and family

know about the good

that you see; it will

help them see it too.

HANOCH McCARTY

FRIENDSHIPS BEGIN
WITH LIKING OR GRATITUDE.

GEORGE ELIOT

I awoke
this morning
with devout
thanksgiving
for my friends,
the old and
the new.

RALPH WALDO EMERSON

Blessed is
the influence of
one true,
loving
human soul
to another.

GEORGE ELIOT

MY FRIENDS
GIVE ME A SENSE,
NOT ONLY OF
WHO I AM,
BUT OF WHAT I TRULY
CAN BECOME.

DAN GARLAND

NOBODY, BUT NOBODY,
CAN MAKE IT OUT HERE ALONE.

MAYA ANGELOU

WE NEED TO THINK OF
OURSELVES AS GIFTS
TO BE GIVEN AND TO
THINK OF OTHERS AS
GIFTS OFFERED TO US.

JOHN POWELL

There are
people who take
the heart out
of you,
and there are
people who
put it back.

ELIZABETH DAVID

MAY HAPPINESS

TOUCH YOUR LIFE TODAY

AS WARMLY AS YOU HAVE

TOUCHED THE LIVES OF OTHERS.

REBECCA FORSYTHE

Ah!

Life grows lovely where you are.

MATHILDE BLIND

You are
not only good
to yourself, but
the cause of
goodness
in others.

SOCRATES

Appreciation is a wonderful thing; it makes what is excellent in others belong to us, as well.

VOLTAIRE

Gratitude

is not only

the greatest

of virtues,

but the

parent of all

the others.

CICERO

Appreciation

in any form

at any time

brightens anyone's

existence.

RUTH STAFFORD PEALE

Appreciative words are the most power-ful force for good on earth.

GEORGE W. CRANE

Gratitude is
the memory
of the heart;
therefore forget
not to say often,
I have all I
ever enjoyed.

LYDIA M. CHILD

FOR ALL THAT HAS BEEN, THANKS.
FOR ALL THAT WILL BE,
YES.

DAG HAMMARSKJOLD

LET NO ONE EVER COME TO YOU WITHOUT LEAVING BETTER.

MOTHER TERESA

Just the simple
kindness of
strangers can mean
everything.

LISA HARLOW

It is in forgetting ourselves
that we are found.

ST. FRANCIS OF ASSISI

I have found that
there is a tremendous
joy in giving.
It is a very
important part of the
joy of living.

WILLIAM BUCK

WHEN YOU CARE, PEOPLE NOTICE.

SUSANE BERGER

Sometimes when I consider what tremendous consequences come from little things, a chance word, a tap on the shoulder...I am tempted to think...there are no little things.

BRUCE BARTON

There is always

something for which

to be thankful.

CHARLES DICKENS

If there is any
kindness I can show,
or any good thing
I can do to
any fellow being,
let me do it now,
and not defer or
neglect it, as I shall
not pass this way again.

WILLIAM PENN

We make a

living by what

we get,

but we make

a life by

what we give.

HENRY BUCHER

Infinite goodness has wide arms.

D A N T E

That best portion of

a good man's life:

His little, nameless,

unremembered acts of

kindness and of love.

WILLIAM WORDSWORTH

WE SHALL
NEVER
KNOW ALL
THE GOOD
THAT
A SIMPLE
SMILE
CAN DO.

MOTHER TERESA

I would maintain
that thanks are
the highest form
of thought, and
that gratitude is
happiness doubled
by wonder.

G. K. CHESTERTON

…it is not joy

that makes us

grateful;

it is gratitude

that makes us

joyful.

BROTHER DAVID STEINDL-RAST

Give thanks
for unknown
blessings
already on
their way.

NATIVE AMERICAN SAYING

GRATITUDE IS ONE OF THE LEAST ARTICULATE OF THE EMOTIONS, ESPECIALLY WHEN IT'S DEEP.

FELIX FRANKFURTER

All we
can ask
in our lives
is that
perhaps we
can make a
little difference
in someone
else's.

LILLIAN DAVIS

Evermore thanks.

WILLIAM SHAKESPEARE

the good life™

Celebrating the joy of living fully.

Also available from Compendium Publishing
are these spirited companion books in The
Good Life series of great quotations:

yes!

refresh

moxie

hero

friend

heart

spirit

success

joy

These books may be ordered directly
from the publisher (800) 914-3327.
But please try your local bookstore first!

www.compendiuminc.com

2011

You are an
amazing friend!
Thank you for your never
ending excitement!